AF597219

WRIGHT

Biography of the Boy from Central City

(Annotated and Illustrated)

RK Vetter with Project Advisor Nancy B. Johnson

First Edition Book, August 2023

Book cover design, illustration, editing, and interior layout by:

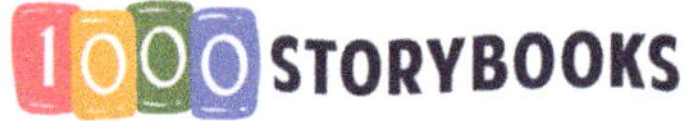

www.1000storybooks.com

DEDICATION

To all, especially Nancy B. Johnson, who have dedicated their efforts to preserving the memory of one of Central City, Nebraska's most famously creative citizens.

One day, Will Morris spied Grace Osborn through the window of the barbershop in Chapman, Nebraska. They were married soon after!

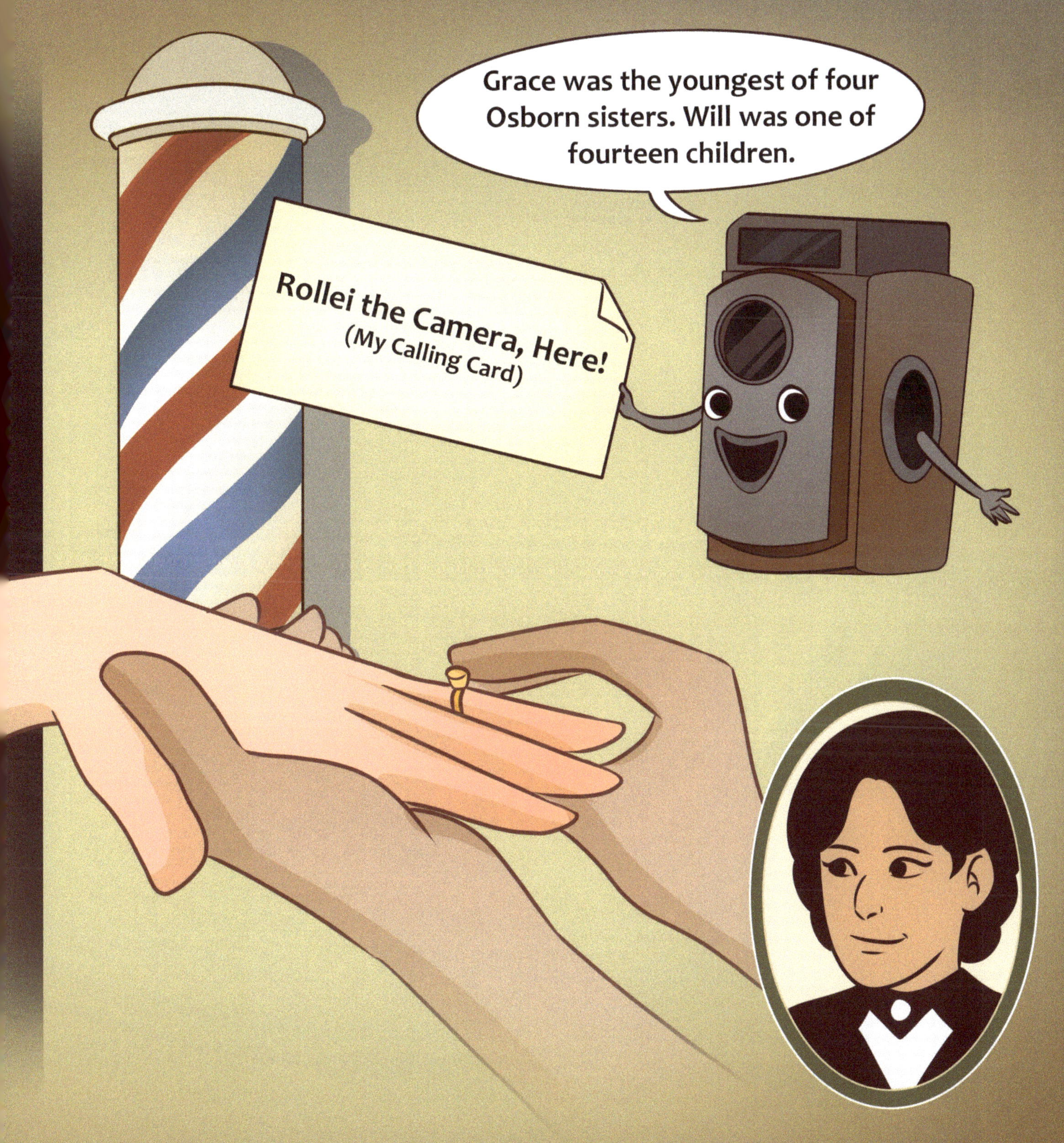
Grace was the youngest of four Osborn sisters. Will was one of fourteen children.
Rollei the Camera, Here!
(My Calling Card)

Will and Grace's boy—Wright—was born on January 6, 1910, in Central City, Nebraska.

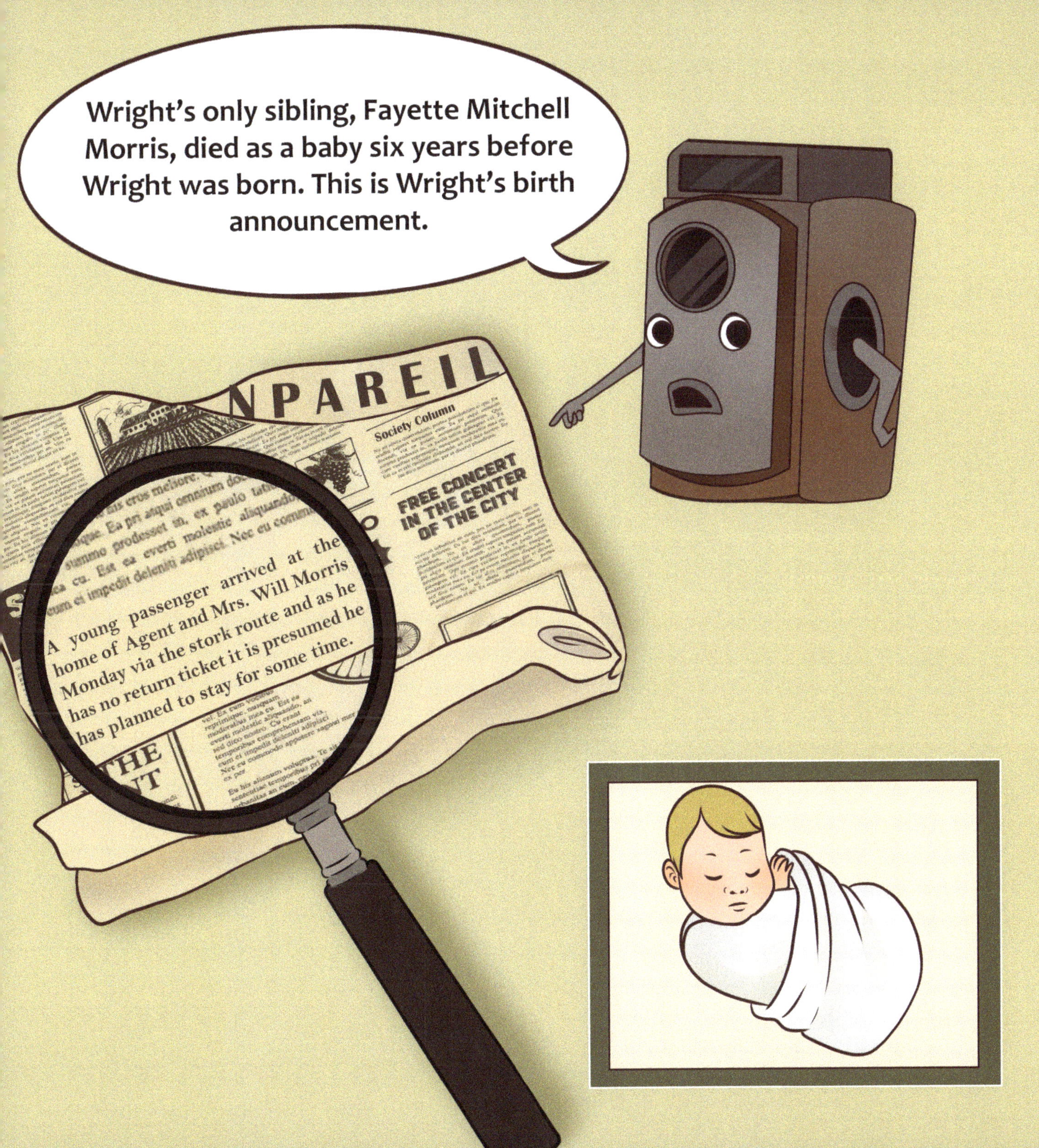
Wright's only sibling, Fayette Mitchell Morris, died as a baby six years before Wright was born. This is Wright's birth announcement.
NPAREIL
Society Column
FREE CONCERT IN THE CENTER OF THE CITY
A young passenger arrived at the home of Agent and Mrs. Will Morris Monday via the stork route and as he has no return ticket it is presumed he has planned to stay for some time.

On Wright's sixth full day of life, Will became his only parent. His mother died, January 13, 1910. Wright's mother, Grace, never got to know her son.

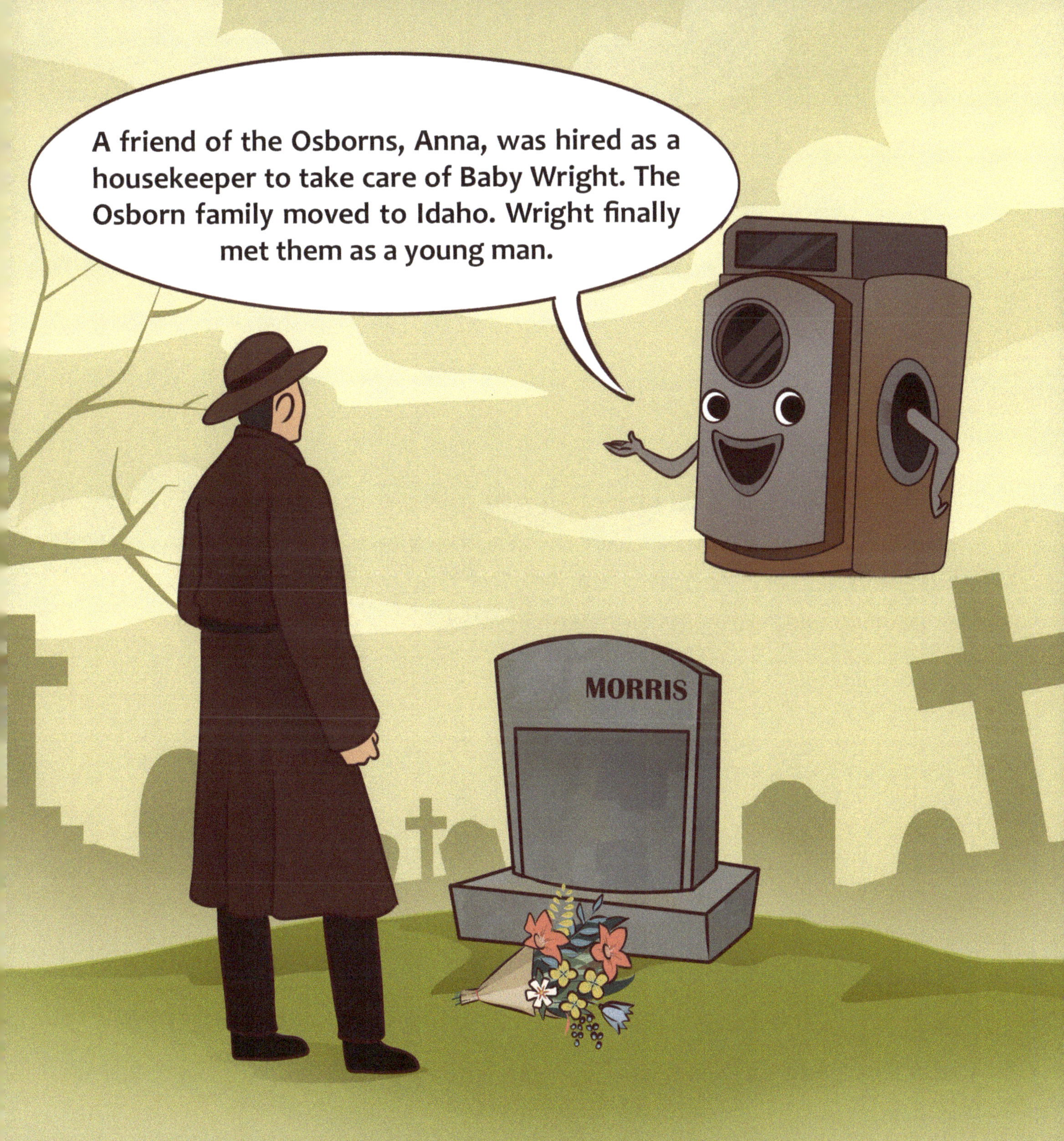
A friend of the Osborns, Anna, was hired as a housekeeper to take care of Baby Wright. The Osborn family moved to Idaho. Wright finally met them as a young man.
MORRIS

And you never got to know Wright, either. But don't you wish you could have been introduced? Wright grew to enjoy viewing his Nebraska life through a variety of frames and appreciating the everyday treasures to be found there.

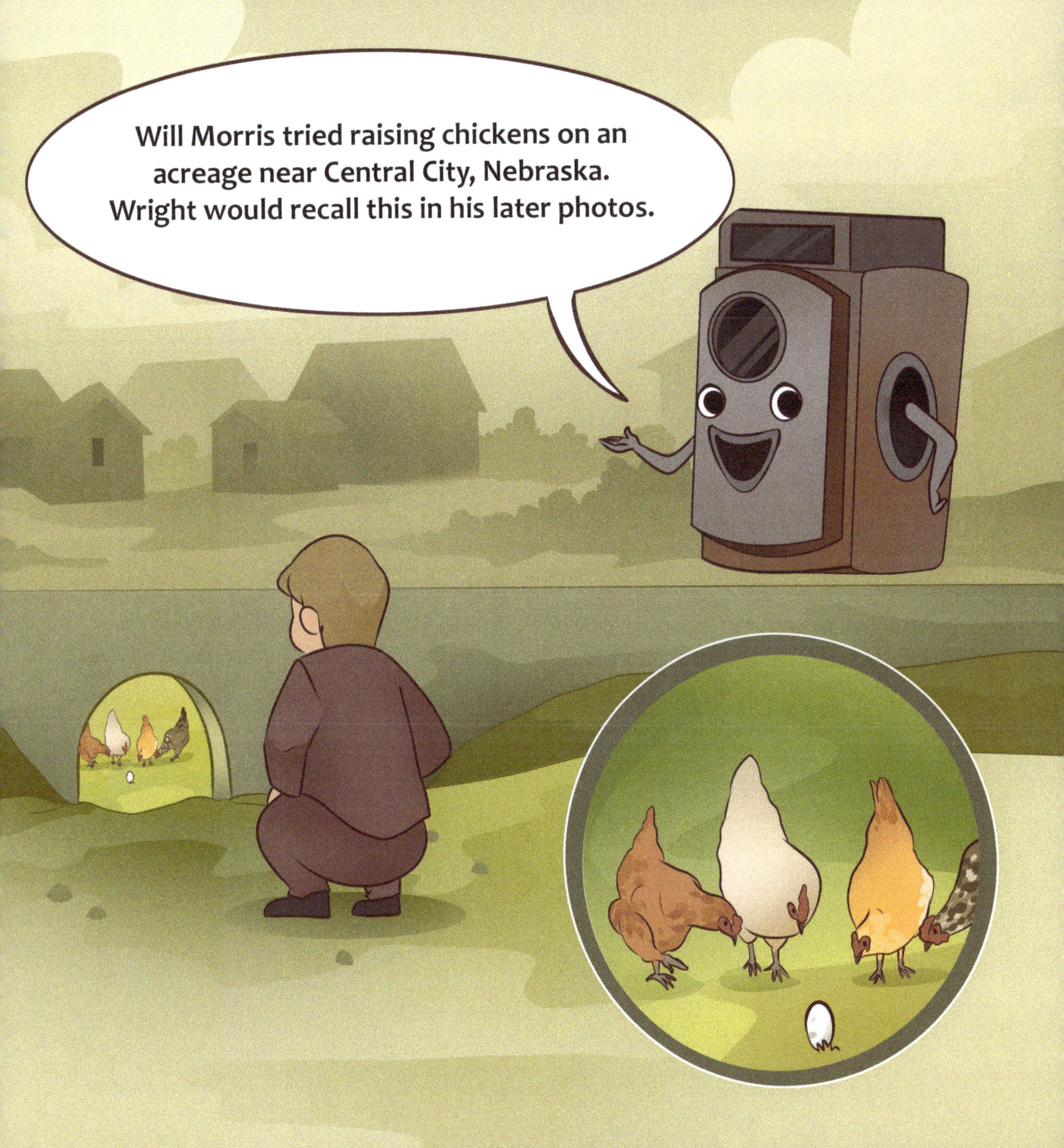
Will Morris tried raising chickens on an acreage near Central City, Nebraska. Wright would recall this in his later photos.

If you and Wright were friends, you may have followed him into the cool dimness under his porch, snapping myriad mental memories of his birth town between the vertical porch slats. You and Wright would have been anonymous observers. He could have taught you how to listen secretly to the voices going past you—and you might have emerged smelling like newly dug potatoes!

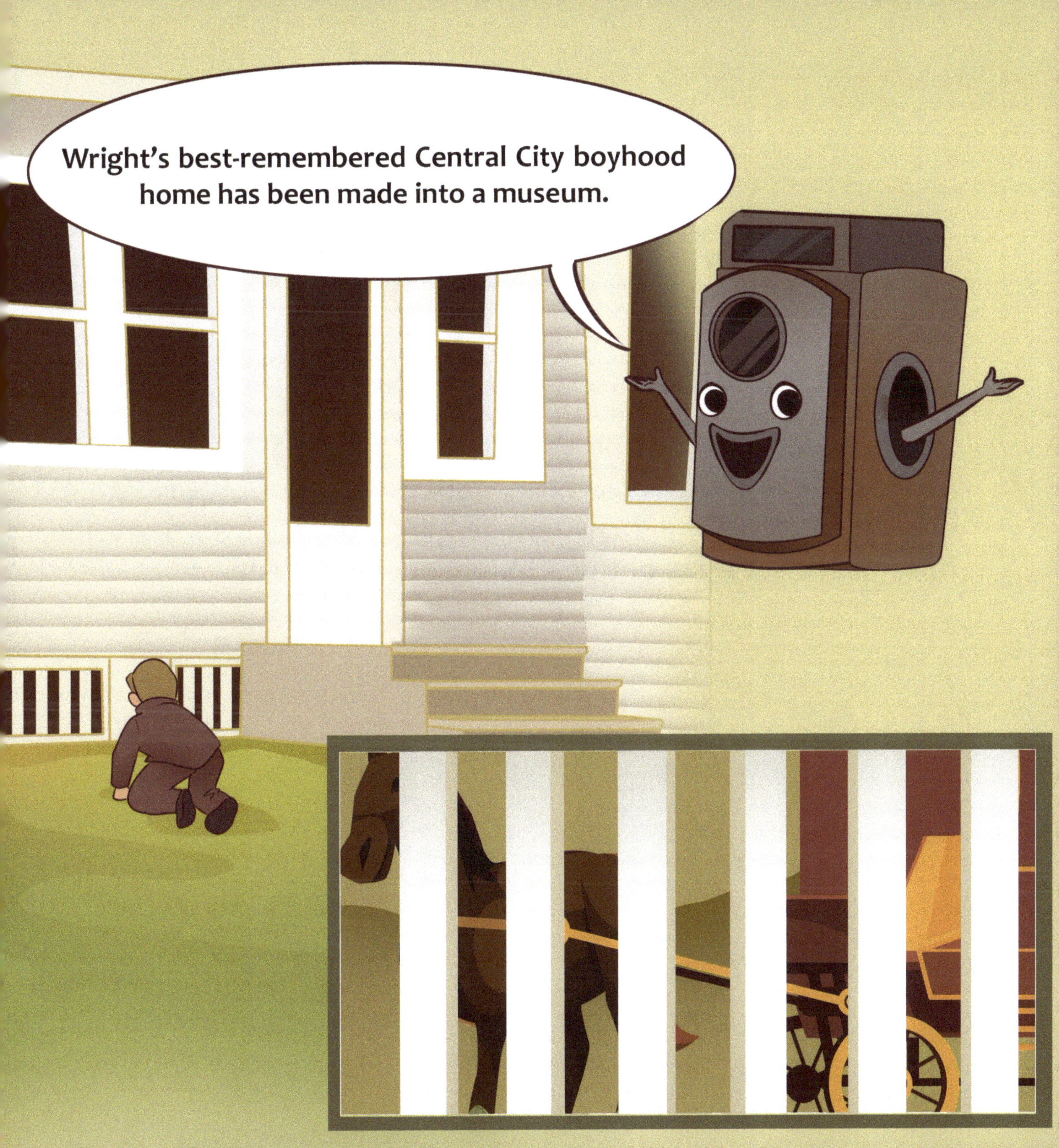
Wright's best-remembered Central City boyhood home has been made into a museum.

Wright's dad worked for the Union Pacific Railroad. Wright's house was only two blocks away from the tracks. You and Wright could have heard the trains thundering through town. You could have felt the quaking of the ground under your feet!

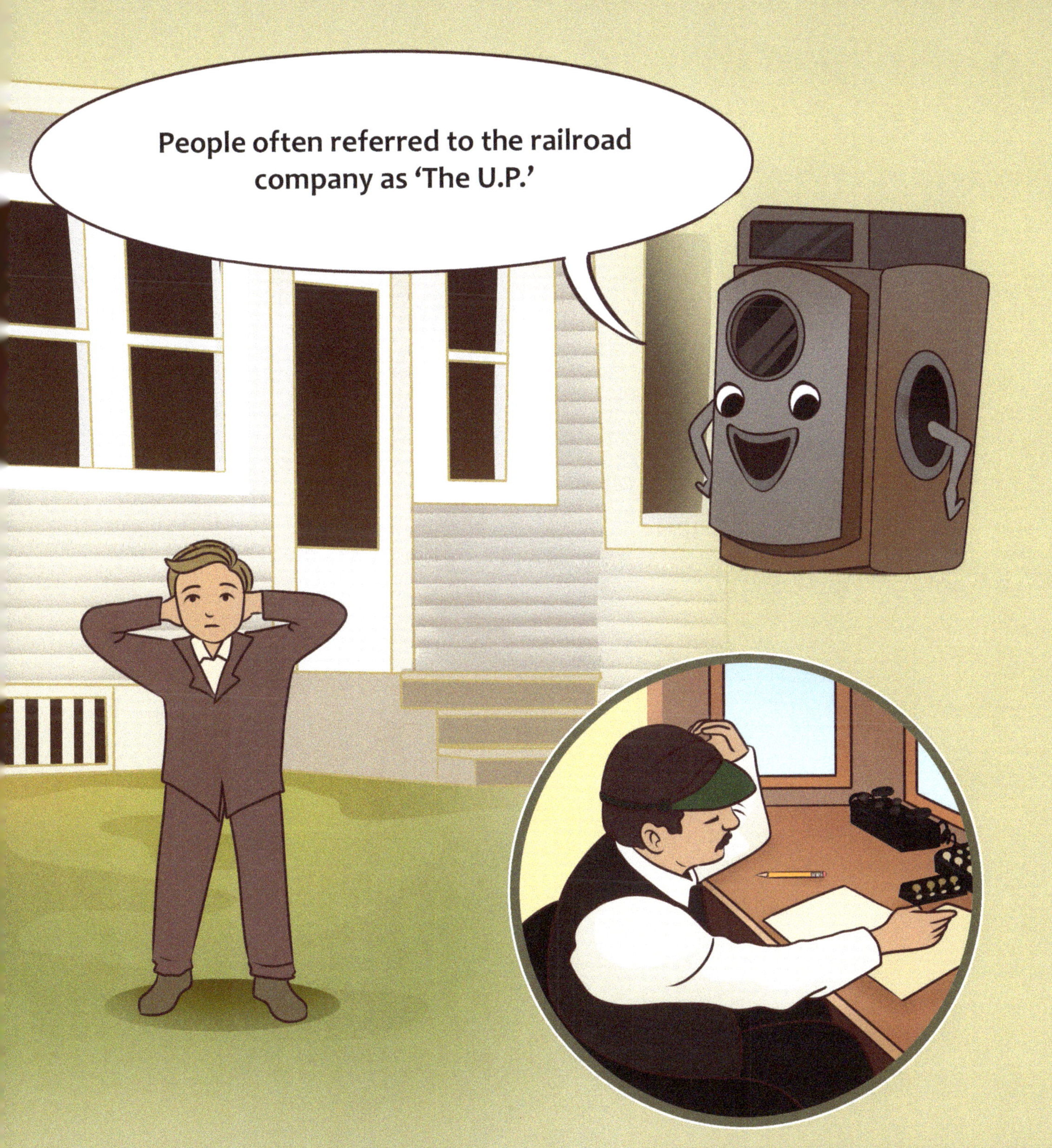
People often referred to the railroad company as 'The U.P.'

Maybe Wright could have taken you inside his house so you could see multihued light coming through the magical, leaded-glass window at just the right time of day.

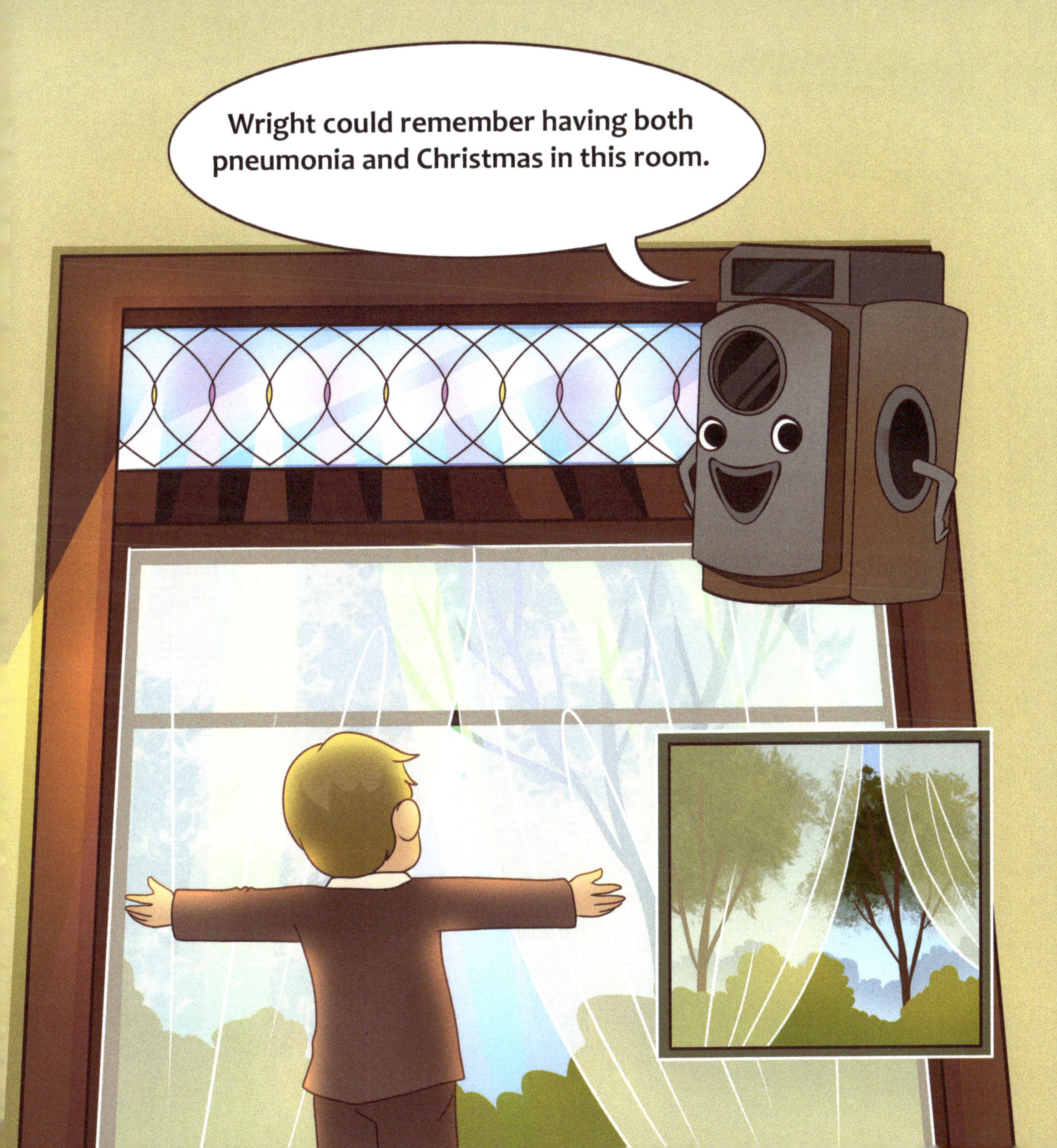
Wright could remember having both pneumonia and Christmas in this room.

Wright may have shown you how to hide under a neighbor's unhitched, braked buggy and witness the world through its smooth wheel spokes. You could smell the hub grease and the worn leather seats above you as you squinted from the dusky undercarriage into the bright light beyond and listened to passing conversations.

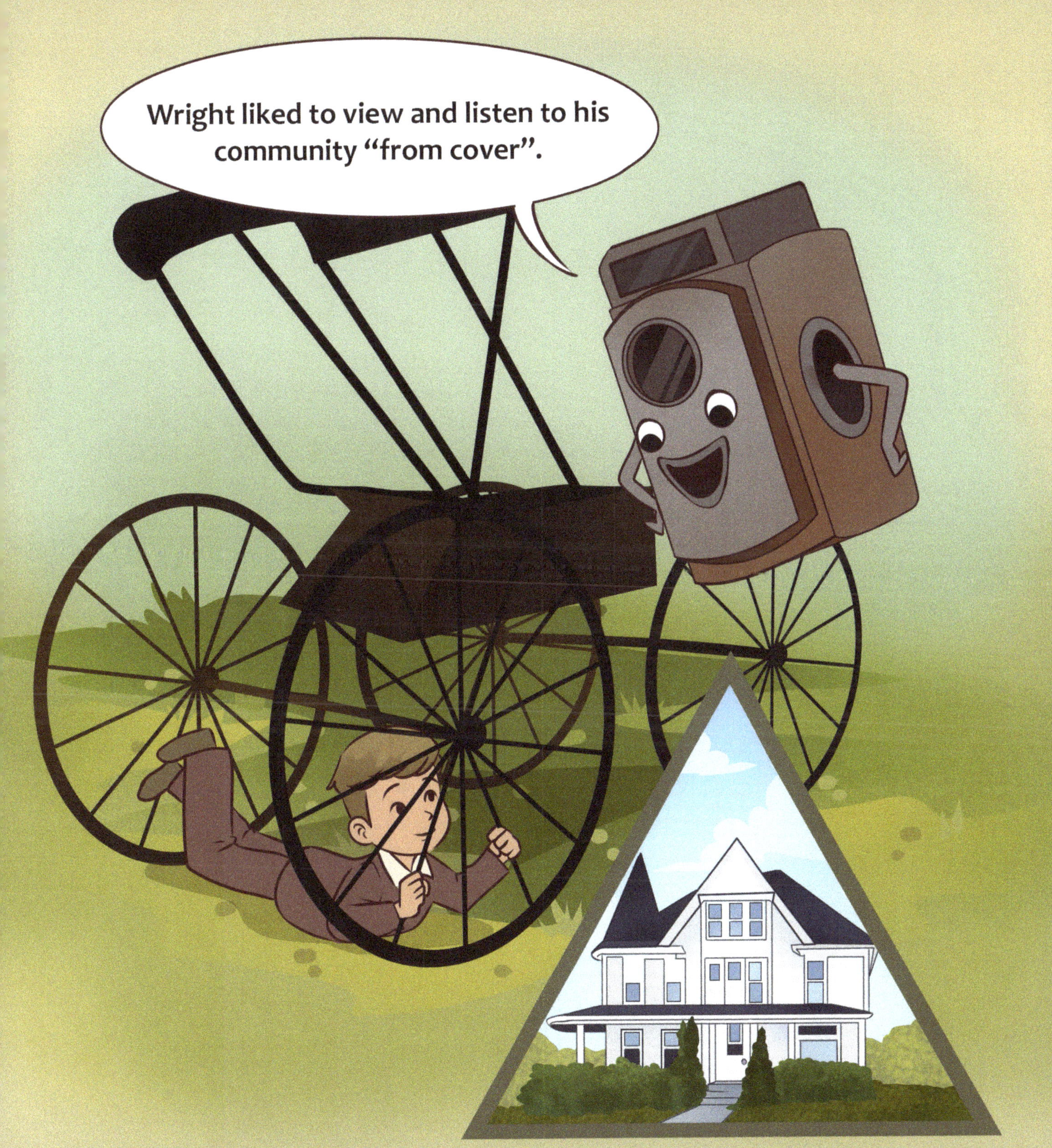
Wright liked to view and listen to his community "from cover".

Perhaps you could have walked with Wright to the new school in his neighborhood. You could have peered through the shiny glass doors of North Ward Elementary, up the darkened main stairway, all the way to the wide windows on the opposite side of the landing.

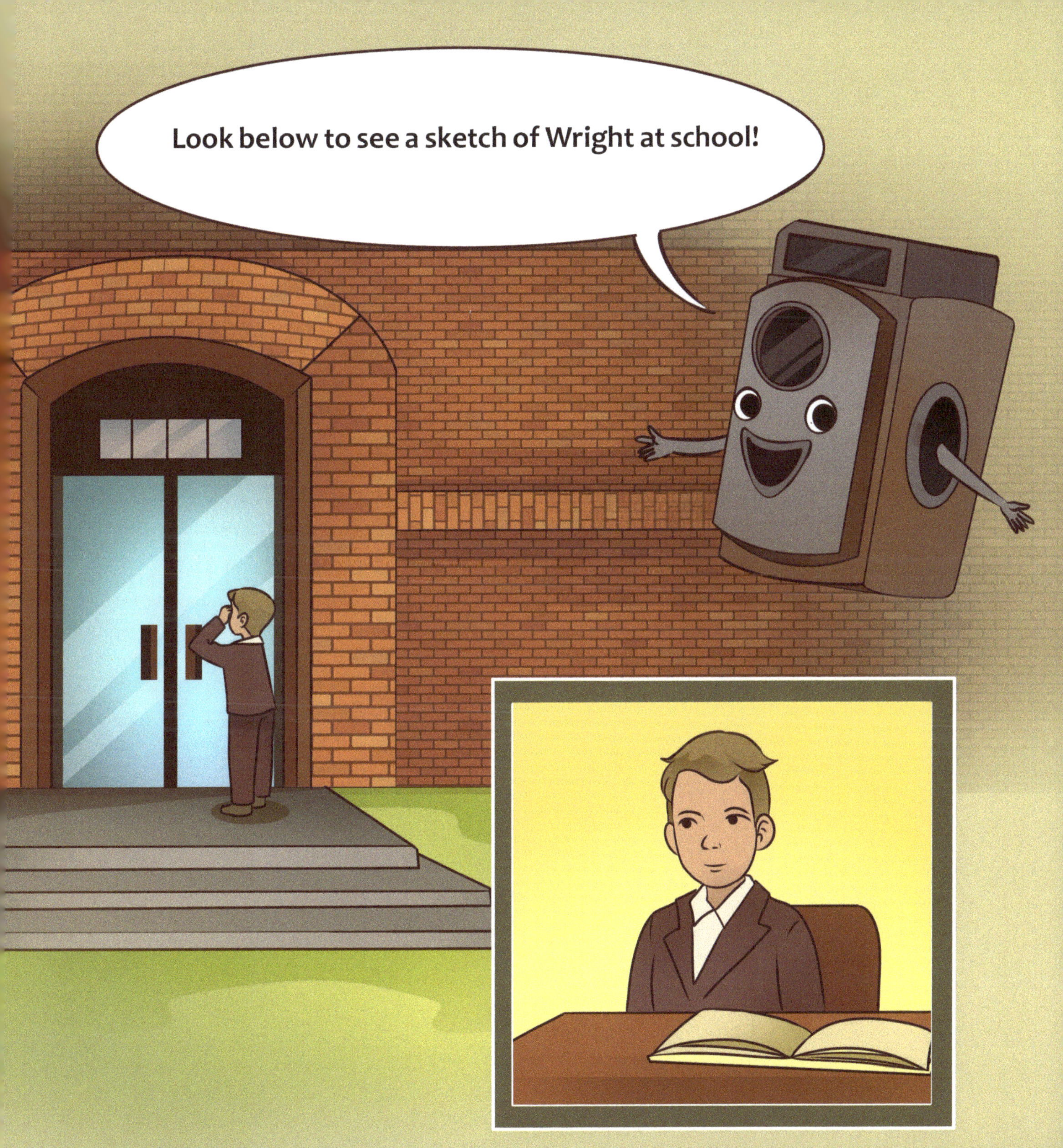
Look below to see a sketch of Wright at school!

Or maybe, you and Wright could have ridden with his dad, Will, in his early 1900s car. You could have seen the hordes of horizontal lines in the wooden bridge that crossed the flat Platte River. You could have caught the scent of sunlit river sand and the shallow river water.

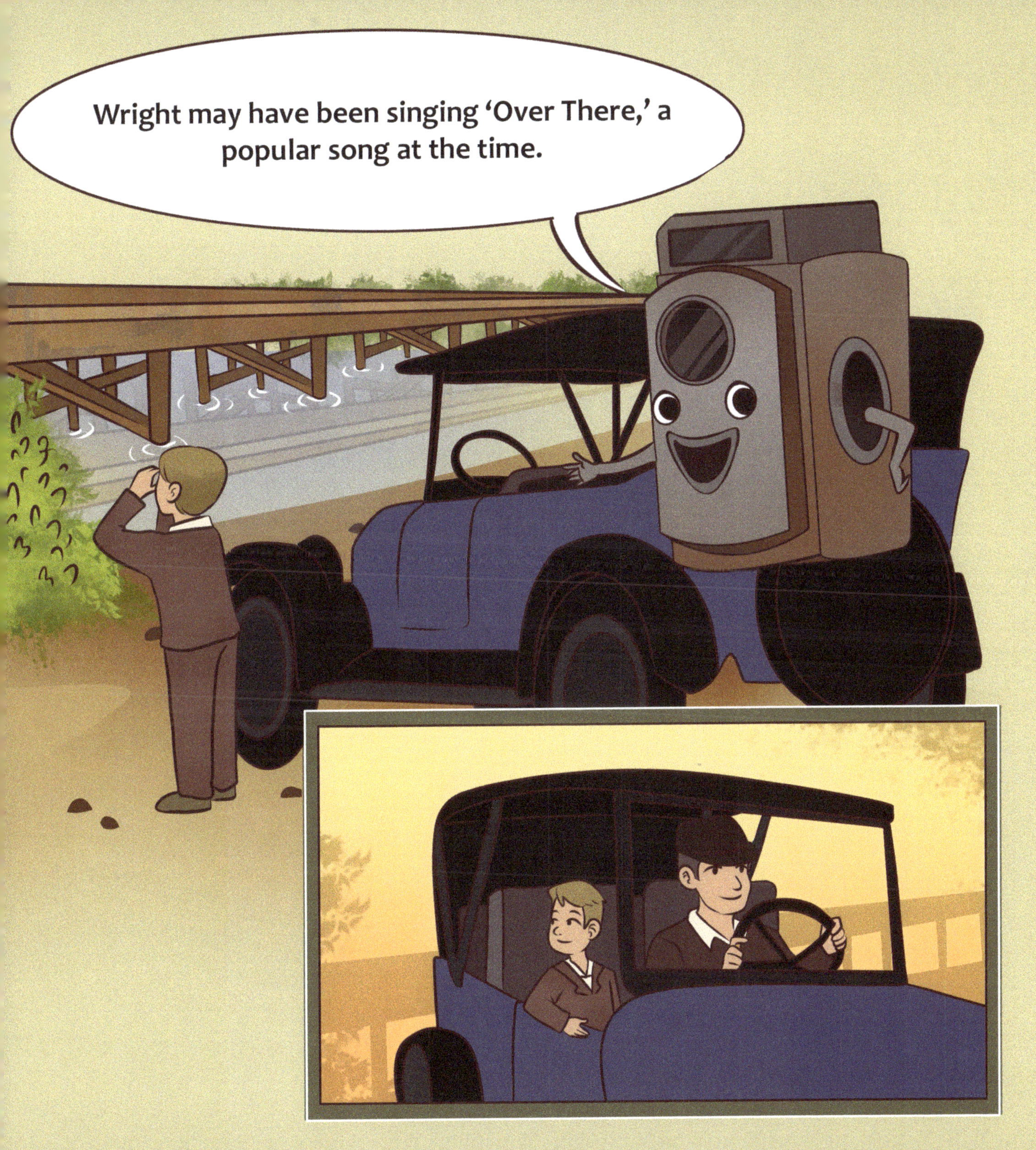
Wright may have been singing 'Over There,' a popular song at the time.

Wright moved away from Central City with his dad and his dad's second wife, Gertrude, when he was nine. During his life, he would live in Omaha, Chicago, California, Pennsylvania, Texas, Mexico, Italy, and Greece.

Wright never forgot about Central City, or Chapman, Nebraska. He came back for visits—especially to the Cahow Barber Shop—where he could reminisce about his younger life spent as "half an orphan" in the area. Wright was buried in 1998 near his mother in Chapman.

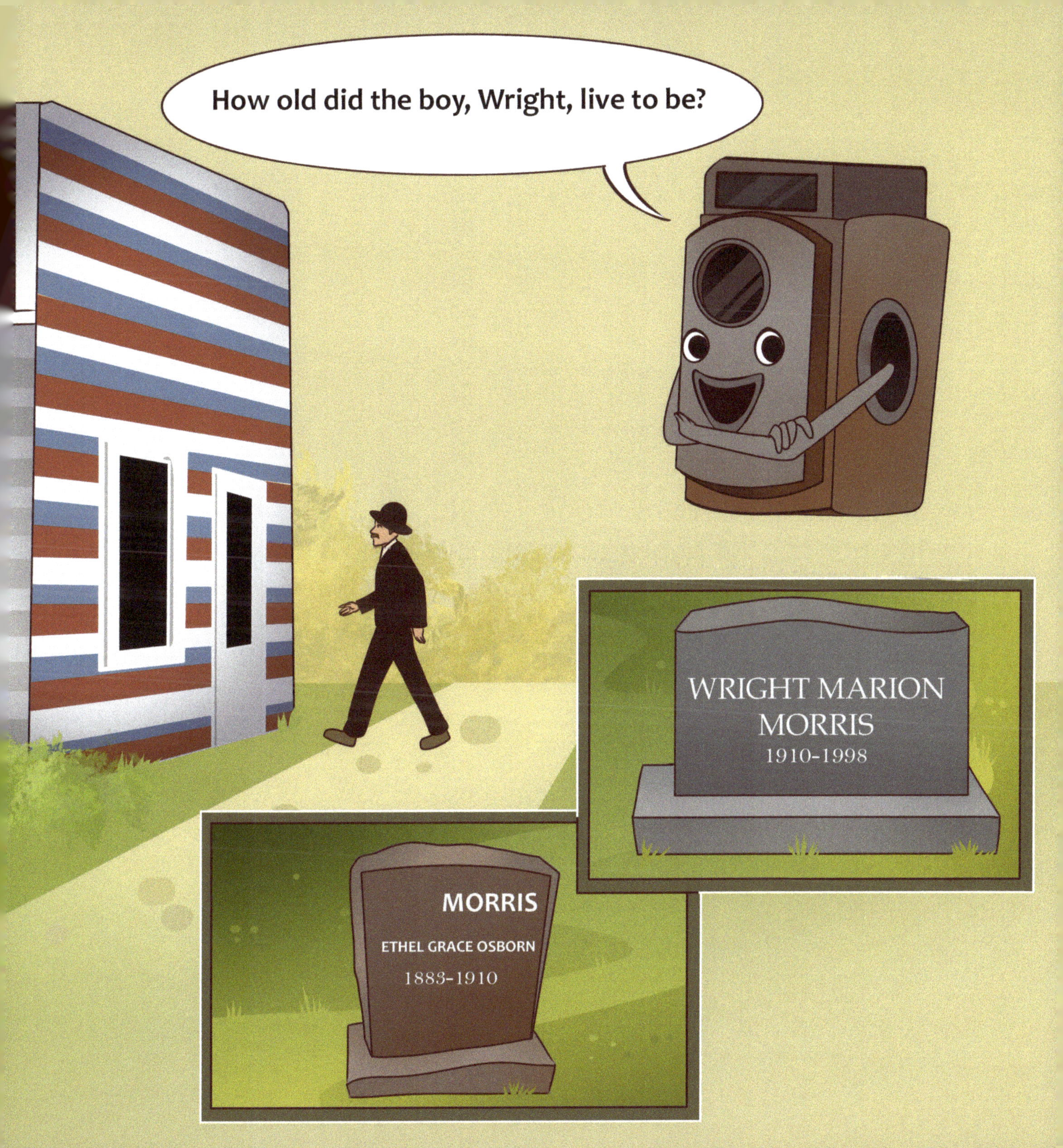
How old did the boy, Wright, live to be?
WRIGHT MARION
MORRIS
1910-1998
MORRIS
ETHEL GRACE OSBORN
1883-1910

As an adult, Wright took world-famous, black-and-white, light-and-shadow photos. It was as though he was still looking through the skirting slats of his porch, the spokes of a buggy, or the culvert near the creek.

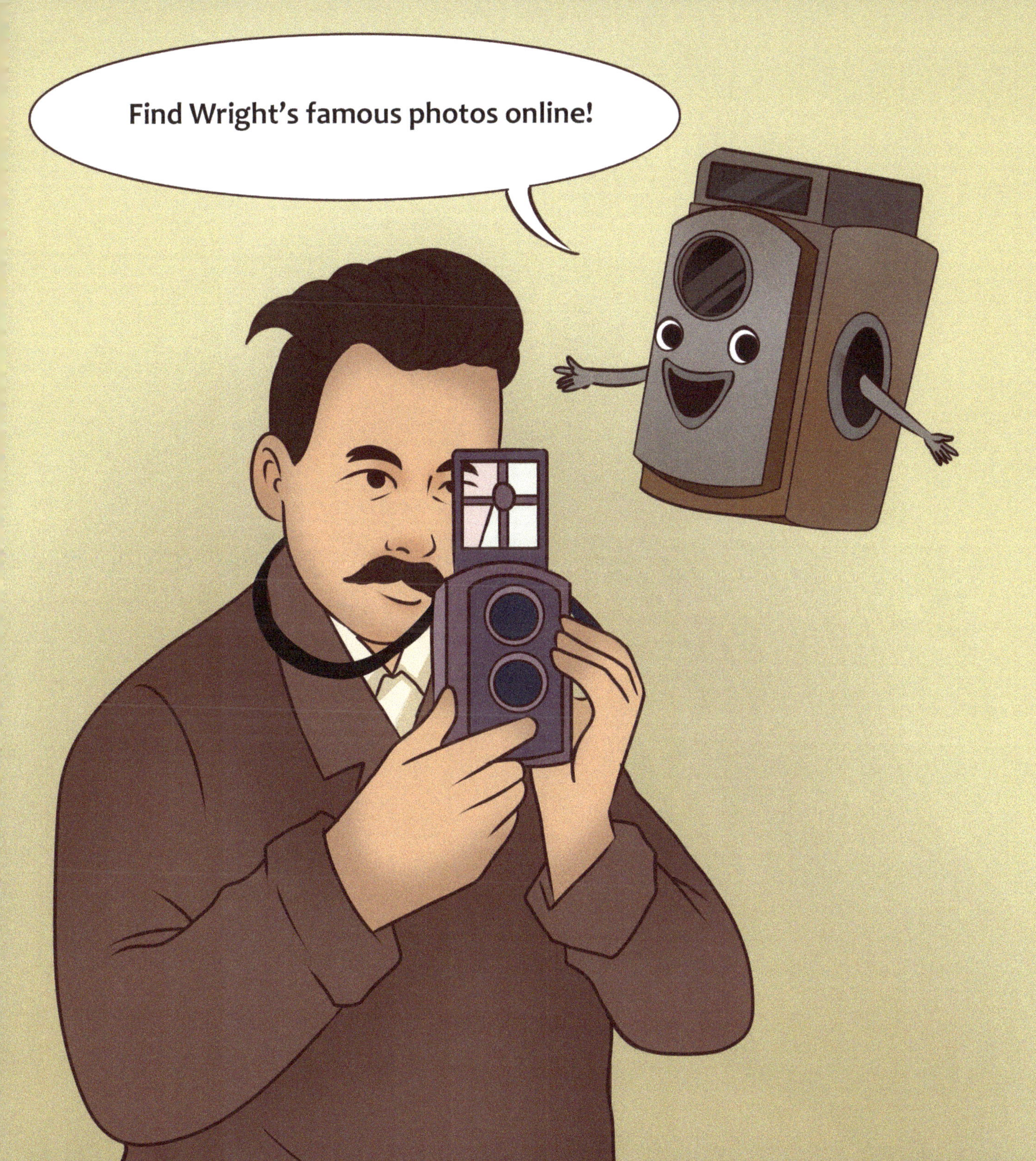
Find Wright's famous photos online!

You never got to know Wright, but don't you wish you could have been introduced? Wright Morris continued to enjoy viewing his world through various lenses. Using his practiced, camera-like eyes, he left many photographs behind for us to enjoy.

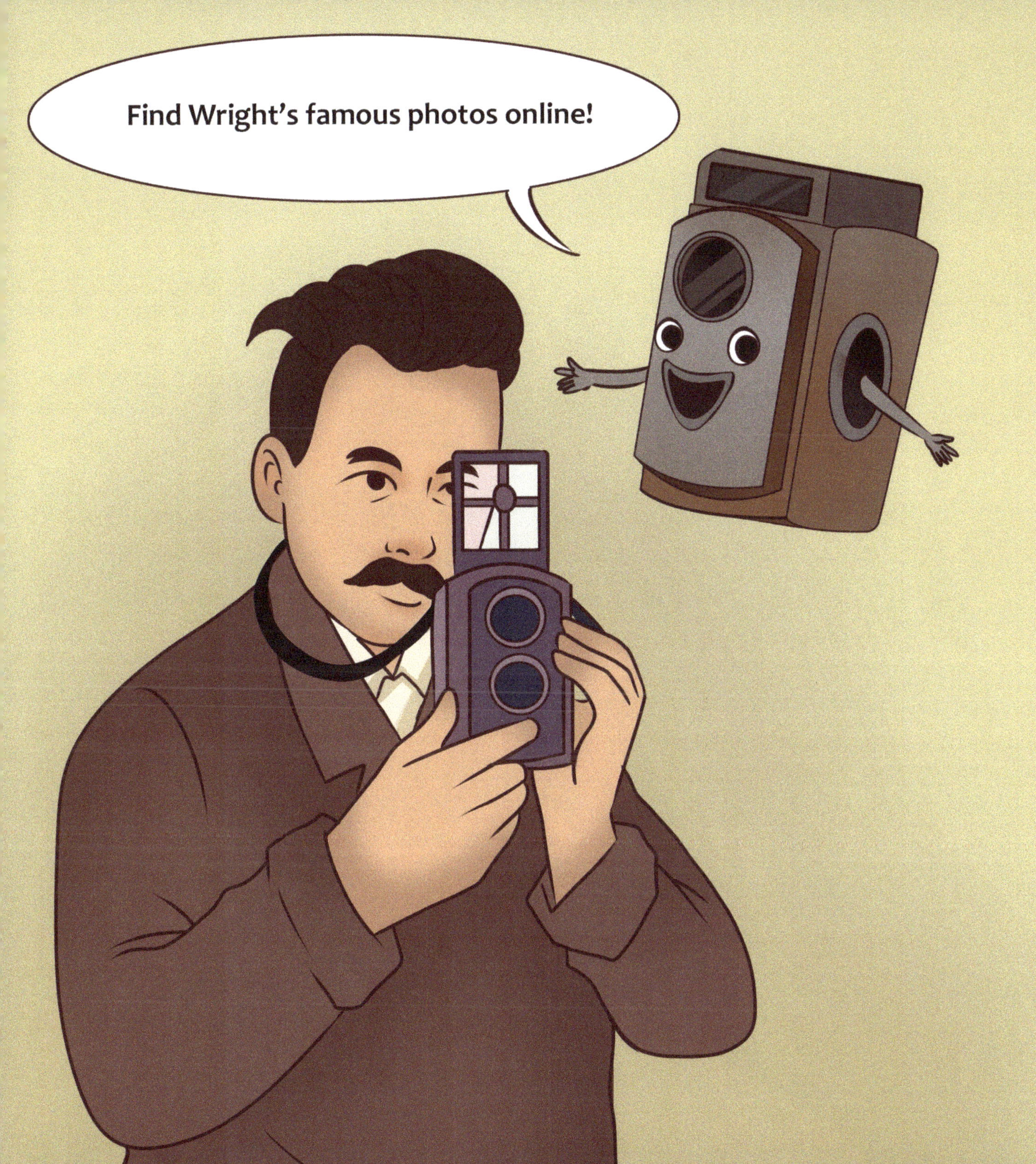
Find Wright's famous photos online!

You never got to know Wright, but don't you wish you could have been introduced? Wright Morris continued to enjoy viewing his world through various lenses. Using his practiced, camera-like eyes, he left many photographs behind for us to enjoy.

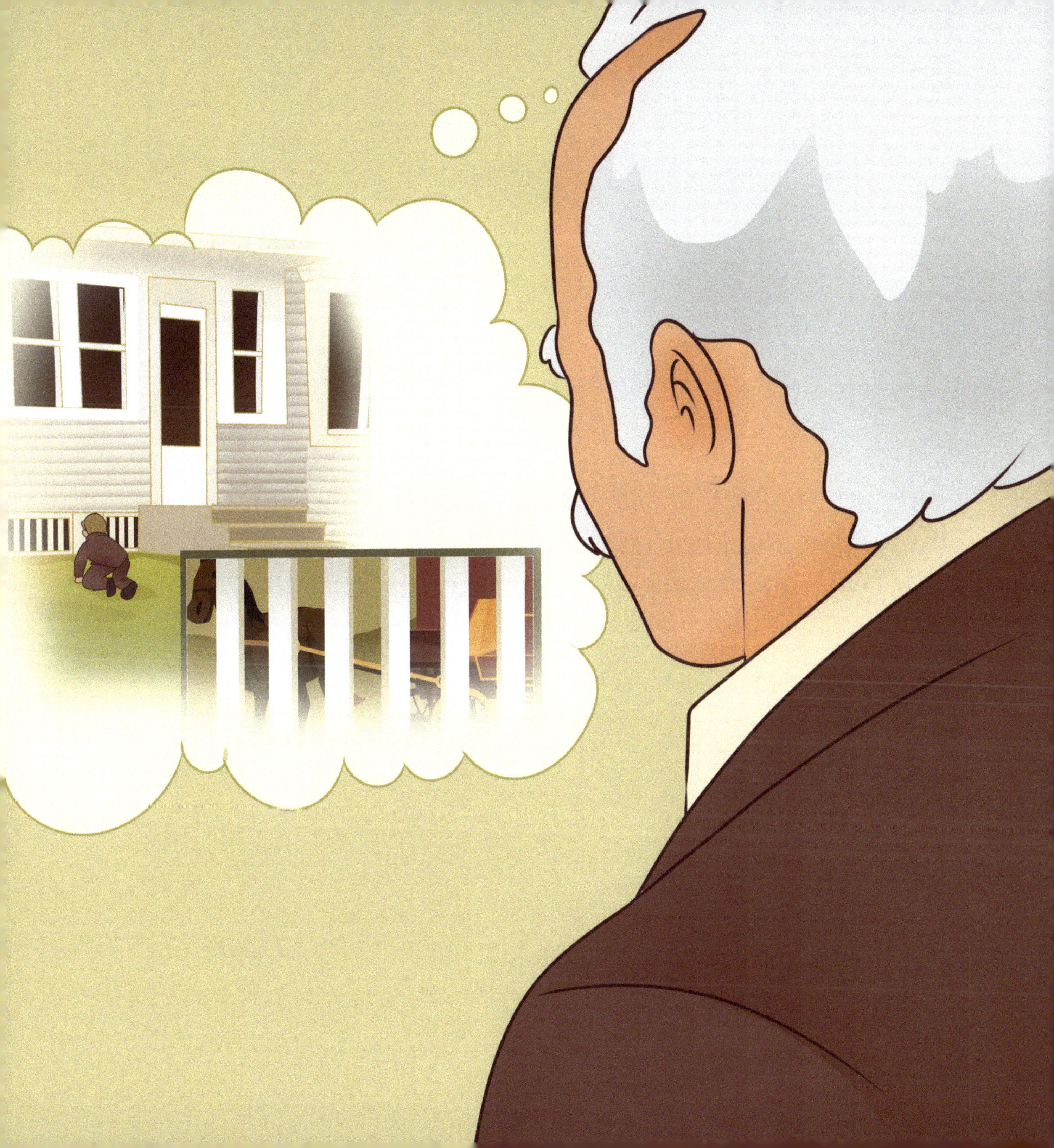

Wright also liked to write. He published many books containing his writing and photographs. He was a world traveler, a college graduate, and a college instructor. He earned many awards, including the National/American Book Award.

Bibliography

Center for Creative Photography, "Wright Morris." n.d. **Wright Morris | Center for Creative Photography (arizona.edu)**, Retrieved 2023-28-03.

Center for Great Plains Studies, "Wright Morris." n.d. **Wright Morris | Center for Great Plains Studies | Nebraska (unl.edu)**, Retrieved 2023-10-03.

Central City Nonpareil, Central City, Nebraska; 13 January 1910. Page 7, Column 1.

The Editors of Encyclopedia Britannica. "National Book Awards: American Literary Award." n.d. **National Book Awards | American literary award | Britannica**, Retrieved 2023-15-03.

Lone Tree Literary Society, Barbara Gorgen, Founder, "From the Childhood Home of Wright Morris." n.d. **Lone Tree Literary Society (wrightmorris.org)**, Retrieved 2023-01-03.

Morris, Wright. **Will's Boy**. United States of America: Penguin Books, 1981

Morris, Wright, Self-Portrait, **The Home Place**, Near Norfolk, Nebraska, 1947

Visit Nebraska, "Wright Morris Boyhood Home." n.d. **Wright Morris Boyhood Home (Central City) | VisitNebraska.com**, Retrieved 2023-11-03.

Reference photos provided by Nancy B. Johnson from her personal collection, the Wright Morris Boyhood Home, and the Morris Family Collection.

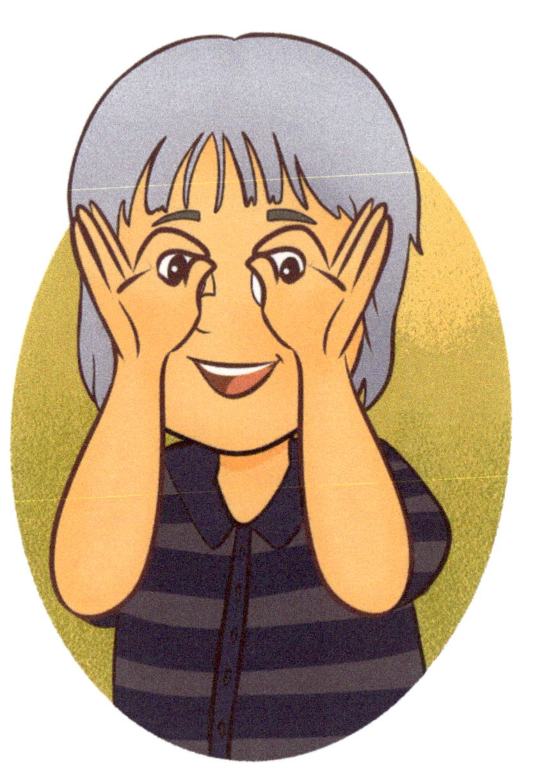

ABOUT THE AUTHOR

RK Vetter grew up on two farms in Iowa, where she began her formal education in two one-room country schools. She taught in Nebraska classrooms for 21 years, is a thirteen-year veteran storytime lady, better known to preschoolers as "Library Kay," and now lives in South Carolina, where she writes, farms her yard, and explores state parks and historical sites.

RK Vetter blogs at rkvetter.wordpress.com, where you can find her other books. RK can also be contacted at vetterrk@gmail.com.

www.ingramcontent.com/pod-product-compliance
Lightning Source LLC
LaVergne TN
LVHW072007150826
845671LV00010B/277
9798988197720